Introducing a Statutory Register of Lobbyists

Consultation Paper

Presented to Parliament
by the Minister for Government Policy
by Command of Her Majesty

January 2012

Cm 8233 £16.00

© Crown copyright 2012

You may re-use this information (excluding logos) free of charge in any format or medium, under the terms of the Open Government Licence. To view this licence, visit http://www.nationalarchives.gov.uk/doc/open-government-licence/ or e-mail: psi@nationalarchives.gsi.gov.uk.

Where we have identified any third party copyright information you will need to obtain permission from the copyright holders concerned.

This publication is available for download at www.official-documents.gov.uk

This document is also available from our website at www.cabinetoffice.gov.uk

ISBN: 9780101823326

Printed in the UK by The Stationery Office Limited on behalf of the Controller of Her Majesty's Stationery Office

ID 2471741   01/12   19585   17729

Printed on paper containing 75% recycled fibre content minimum.

Foreword

The Coalition Government is committed to introducing a statutory register of lobbyists. The Government already releases a significant amount of information at www.data.gov.uk. But we need to go further; a statutory register of lobbyists is an important step towards making politics more transparent. We are determined to keep working to open up politics, to make it more accessible to everyone.

Lobbying serves an important function in politics – by putting forward the views of stakeholders to policy makers, it helps in the development of better legislation. But it needs to be open and transparent.

Members of the public, MPs and campaigners have written to us over the last eighteen months, expressing their views on what should be included in a register of lobbying activity. This consultation is intended to draw out all of those views and more. But we need you to help us - we want interested parties, individuals and businesses to tell us what they think a register should look like. How would you define a 'lobbyist'? What sort of information should be held on a register? What sort of penalties should be in place if you don't register?

Responses can be submitted in writing or electronically and the Government will publish a summary of consultation responses once the consultation is closed. I hope as many people as possible will respond over the next twelve weeks, making sure that every voice is heard.

Oliver Letwin MP
Minister for Government Policy

Mark Harper MP
Minister for Political and Constitutional Reform

Contents

1. Introduction	7
2. Consultation Details	8
3. Purpose of the UK statutory register	9
4. Questions for consultation:	12
Definitions;	12
Information to be included in the register;	14
How often should the register be updated;	15
Should there be any additional functions linked to the register;	15
How should the register be funded;	16
What sanctions would be appropriate	16
Who should run the register?	17
5. Summary of questions	18
Annex A:	20
1. Background	20
2. Examples of current practice in other jurisdictions	23
3. Examples of current practice in current UK registers	28
Annex B: Code of Practice on Consultation	30

1. Introduction

The Government is committed to introducing a statutory register of lobbyists. Following the May 2010 election, the Government said, in The Coalition: Our Programme for Government:

> *We will regulate lobbying through introducing a statutory register of lobbyists and ensuring greater transparency.*[1]

The Government's aim is to increase the information available about lobbyists without unduly restricting lobbyists' freedom and ability to represent the views of the businesses, groups, charities and other individuals and organisations they represent or to deter members of the public from getting involved in policy making.

This paper asks a number of specific questions whose answers will help inform the drafting of the legislation that will be brought forward to meet the Government's commitment. Responses to these questions, and any other points you think relevant to legislation to create a statutory register of lobbyists, are invited by 13 April 2012. The Government will take all responses and suggestions into account before bringing forward legislation, which will be fully debated by Parliament before it becomes law.

---

[1] *The Coalition: Our programme for government*, Section 16 Government Transparency, pg 21. Available from: www.cabinetoffice.gov.uk/media/409088/pfg_coalition.pdf

2. Consultation Details

Purpose

The purpose of this consultation is to give all interested parties the opportunity to comment on the policy options that will underpin the establishment of a statutory register of lobbyists.

Timetable

The consultation will run for 12 weeks from 20 January 2012. The Government will consider all responses received by 13 April 2012.

How to respond

Please send your comments and views to:

>Statutory Register of Lobbyists
>Area 4/S1
>1 Horse Guards Road
>London SW1A 2HQ

Alternatively, please email your response to registerlobbyists@cabinet-office.gsi.gov.uk marking your response with **Statutory Register of Lobbyists** in the subject field of your email.

Should you require this document or the consultation response template in a different format, please advise us of your specific requirements by contacting us at registerlobbyists@cabinet-office.gsi.gov.uk.

Confidentiality

The Government may pass the information you send to colleagues within the Cabinet Office and other government departments. The Government may also publish your comments in a summary of responses to this consultation. The Government will assume that you are content with this and, when replying by email, your consent overrides any confidentiality disclaimer that is generated by your organisation's IT system unless you specifically include a request to the contrary in the main text of your response.

3. Purpose Of The UK Statutory Register

Lobbying – seeking to influence public policy, government decisions or legislation - can improve results by ensuring that those developing and considering the options are better informed about the consequences of the available options. Lobbying is a perfectly legitimate activity that has been carried out for many years in many different forums by a wide variety of individuals and groups of all sorts. However, where lobbying is not transparent, it can undermine public confidence in the decision-making process and its results.

The Government asks a number of questions in the next section on the definition of lobbying and the scope and management of the register. However there are some points on which the Government does not propose to consult.

The purpose of the UK register is to increase transparency by making available to the public, to decision-makers and to other interested parties authoritative and easily-accessible information about who is lobbying and for whom. This will help ensure that those seeking to influence decisions do so in a way that is open to scrutiny, improving knowledge about the process and the accountability of those involved in it.

But the register is not intended to capture or deter a range of activity that is essential to a vibrant democracy. So, for example, the register is not intended to cover the normal interaction between constituents and their MPs. Nor should the essential flow of communication between business leaders and Government, civil figures, community organisations and Government and so on, be included.

The Government already publishes quarterly information about Ministers' meetings. Information about which stakeholders are meeting Ministers to put forward their views on policies is therefore already in the public domain. But under the current system, when Ministers meet lobbying firms it is not transparent on whose behalf they are lobbying.

The Government does not wish to create an obstacle to necessary interaction with policy makers or an undue burden on those who work as lobbyists or employ lobbyists. At the end of this process of consultation and following consideration of the responses, the Government envisages introducing legislation to create a statutory register, run by a body independent of government, which collects information on lobbyists and their clients.

The Government believes that the result of the consultative process should be a set of proposals which create a register which is a proportionate and considered response to public concerns about the lack of transparency in the lobbying industry. It should increase transparency without stifling the useful input into policy making provided by lobbyists. A register should be a public record of who is lobbying and for whom, not a complete regulator for the industry.

The Government believes this should be sufficient to address concerns about a lack of transparency. It does not believe that there should be a statutory code of conduct for lobbyists linked with the register. This would potentially impose costly and unnecessary regulation on the industry, their clients, and the Government.

The Government's initial proposals for consultation are set out below. The next section of this consultation paper discusses in more detail the reasons for these proposals.

How a register might work

A lobbying firm would be required to update the register quarterly with:

- registered address of the company and Company Number
- names of employees engaged in lobbying
- whether those employees are former ministers or senior civil servants
- client lists

This should be no more burdensome than filling out an online form.

A self-employed lobbyist would be required to update the register quarterly with his details and his client list.

Members of the public accessing the register should be able to easily see details of lobbying firms and their employees, as well as who has employed those lobbying firms. Because Government departments already publish lists of their external meetings there is no need to provide further information about specific contacts with Government.

Definition

- Lobbyists should mean those who undertake lobbying activities on behalf of a third party client or whose employees conduct lobbying activities on behalf of a third party client.

- It may also include certain other categories of person following consultation.

- It should <u>not</u> mean those who engage in lobbying activities on their own behalf rather than for a client.

Information

- The information on the register should consist of the company registration details; the names of those persons employed, contracted or otherwise engaged to carry out lobbying and whether that person is a former Minister or senior civil servant.

- The information should also include a list of clients on whose behalf the lobbyist carries out lobbying activities.

- The information might also include limited financial information.

- It should not include details of meetings with Ministers, which are already made available by each Government Department on www.data.gov.uk

Scope

- A register should include those who lobby the UK Government and UK Parliament.

- We will now be taking forward discussions with a view to including the Devolved Administrations and Legislatures within the scope of a statutory register.

4. Questions For Consultation

The key questions for this consultation exercise are:

- The definitions of *lobbying* and *lobbyists*;

- Who should and should not be required to register;

- What information should be provided in the register;

- How often should the register be updated;

- How should the register be funded;

- What sanctions might be appropriate;

- Who should run the register?

Definitions

The scope of the register will in large part be set by the final definition of lobbying and lobbyist. There is presently a definition of lobbying and lobbyists which was created by the UK Public Affairs Council (UKPAC) for use in their voluntary register. The UK Public Affairs Council was created by the three main industry bodies, as an independent institution, tasked with maintaining a voluntary register, as a response to the recommendations of the Public Administration Select Committee (PASC) report on lobbying in 2009. More detail on the operation of UKPAC and the voluntary register can be found in Annex A. The definition was created for use with this voluntary register following internal consultations within the industry.

The UKPAC definitions currently have effect in respect of a voluntary register, which is not backed by statute and which is not open to legal interpretation or challenge in the same way that a definition enshrined in law would be. A discussion of this definition can be found in Annex A, part 1, but the Government does not feel it is appropriate for a statutory register. This is because we feel it does not strike the right distinction between professional lobbying and activity and normal interaction between individuals or businesses with Government Ministers and officials, and Parliamentarians.

The Lobbying Disclosure Act in the United States of America excludes from its definition of a lobbyist anyone whose lobbying activity takes up less than 20 per cent of their working time over a three-month period. Problems have been reported with the operation of this exemption. Difficulties include knowing when the 20 per cent threshold is passed and encouraging people seeking to keep their lobbying secret to claim they were offering services – such as legal, communications or strategic advice – and not lobbying. A similar threshold is not proposed for the UK register.

A definition along the lines of that in the Australian Lobbying Register might be more appropriate. That definition can be found in Annex A, part 2, but in brief it limits the requirement to register to those lobbying on behalf of a third party, with a wide range of exclusions for charities, church groups and other organisations.

This definition has a focus on what is not covered by the register and raises a number of questions about exemptions to the duty to register in the UK.

- Should in-house lobbyists be covered? Many large companies have employees whose main duties are to lobby on behalf of that company. The Government proposes that only those lobbying on behalf of third parties should be covered by the Register. Given that is clear whose interests they represent, it is not evident that an extension of the register to in-house lobbyists would provide any additional transparency.

- Should lobbyists or firms acting on a pro bono basis have an exemption from the duty to register?

- Should organisations which engage in lobbying on behalf of interest groups such as Think Tanks and Charities be required to register? If so, how might this be captured in the definition of lobbying or lobbyist?

- The Government does not wish to discourage the normal activity between constituents and MPs. Should there be an explicit exemption included in any definition?

Trade unions may have an interest in government policies or other issues of the day. It is not unusual for trade unions to campaign on behalf of their members in favour of particular public policies. Some trade unions maintain a political fund. This is a separate account which the trade union can use to provide financial support for a political party. For example, they could donate to a party or particular politician, produce leaflets in support at an election, or support any party conference costs.

- Should Trade Unions be required to register? If so, how might this be captured in the definition of lobbying or lobbyist?

Government

Those working within government, whether the UK government, devolved administrations or local government, are often involved in negotiations over the impact of initiatives or services, for example to make sure that the needs of a particular community are properly taken into account. Few would consider this amounted to lobbying but, for the sake of clarity, it is proposed that discussions between different arms or levels of government should not trigger a requirement to register.

The revised Code of Recommended Practice on Local Authority Publicity[2] makes it clear that Councils should not spend taxpayers' money to lobby Government through private sector lobbyists.

The document 'Rules on Lobbying for Non Departmental Public Bodies'[3] states that Non-departmental Public Bodies must never employ external firms or consultants to influence or attempt to influence Parliament, Government or political parties.

The Government is interested in hearing your views on the definitions to be used for the register. The Government's intention is to increase transparency without adversely affecting normal public participation in the development of Government policy. Do you have any comments as to how the proposals might adversely affect public participation or how public participation can best be safeguarded? Do you agree with the proposed inclusions and exemptions? If not, why not? What do you suggest instead? What do you think the impact of registration on lobbyists and lobbying firms might be? Will it adversely affect the industry?

Information to be included in the register

The Government's overall approach towards regulation is that it should be carried out only where it is clearly justified and, where it is, it should keep the requirements to a minimum in order to avoid creating unnecessary burdens or costs. The Government believes a statutory register is justified and that making the process as simple and straightforward as possible will both encourage participation and minimise burdens. The Ministerial Code contains a requirement at 8.14 to publish, at least quarterly, details of Ministers' external meetings.

Our initial proposal is that a register should include information about the names of individual lobbyists and lobbying firms and the names of their clients. In addition, we propose that the register should include whether a lobbyist was previously a Government Minister or a Senior Civil Servant. The Government does not propose that any information on meetings should be included in a register. Details of meetings between Ministers and third parties are already published regularly, and the Government feels the provision of duplicate information in a statutory register of lobbyists is unnecessary.

Financial information

Some believe that financial information, for example, how much a lobbyist is paid to represent a certain interest, should be published in the register.

While this would undoubtedly shine extra light on lobbying activity, the Government is not persuaded that requiring financial information would be justified. It is more important to know who is lobbying and for whom than to know the cost. Significant difficulties could arise from the need to provide financial information. It might also force companies to reveal sensitive commercial information, for example, that different clients were charged different rates, which could undermine their business.

For these reasons, the Government is not proposing at this stage to require *detailed* financial information but is interested in your views on whether information should be required on the broad value of the work carried out. For example, registrants could declare that they received remuneration in bands indicating the overall scale of the services they are providing. MPs are required to give details of

---

[2] http://www.communities.gov.uk/publications/localgovernment/publicitycode2011
[3] http//www.cabinetoffice.gov.uk/sites/default/files/resources/ndpbs-lobbying.pdf

remuneration, for any outside activities, in bands of £5000, e.g. £0-5,000, £5,001-£10,000 etc. Would this system be appropriate or would it place an undue burden on those required to register?

The Government is interested in your views on this issue. In particular, if you favour the inclusion of financial information, what would be the best ways of safeguarding commercial sensitivities and keeping down the cost and burden of providing the information to the absolute minimum?

The European Transparency Register requires registrants to declare the amount and source of any funding received from EU institutions. **The Government proposes that UK lobbyists should have a similar responsibility, and intends to require them to declare what public funding they have received and from what source** in the most recently completed financial year at the time of initial registration or of renewal. This will help ensure that the public know more about the way in which its money is spent. Do you agree with this proposal?

How often should the register be updated?

US lobbying legislation requires quarterly returns. Canada's requires some aspects to be updated every month while the European Transparency Register is updated only annually. Meanwhile, in the UK, Ministers are required to publish information on gifts (received or given), hospitality, travel and meetings with external organisations on a quarterly basis. **Our initial proposal is that quarterly updates should also apply to the information held in the register of lobbyists.**

Do you agree with these proposals? If not, why not? What do you suggest instead?

Should there be any additional functions linked to the register?

There is a choice to be made as to how active the operator of the register should be in respect of the information it contains. For example, should the operator have the responsibility for verifying the information received, or for investigating anomalies or suspected non-disclosures?

The Government proposes that the operator should, in conjunction with the industry and other interested parties, including, for example, representatives of the media and of groups seeking greater freedom of information, decide on the format or formats in which information is to be provided and published. The operator should take reasonable steps to check that it has accurately reproduced the information those registering have supplied, and work with them to improve the overall quality and usefulness of their entries. However, ultimate responsibility for the information published should lie with those required to register and not the register's operator. For this reason, it is not proposed that the operator should be given the responsibility or power to carry out investigations or audits of the information for publication.

The Government notes that UKPAC's key functions include a number that relate to the conduct of lobbying. In its report on lobbying, PASC called for a code of conduct for lobbyists.

The Government supports the industry's efforts to improve lobbying practice, and to develop a code of conduct that helps lobbyists perform to the highest possible standards. However, it thinks that this is a matter for the industry itself, not for the operator of the register. The register should be a register of activity, not a complete regulator for the industry.

Do you agree with these proposals? If not, why not? What do you suggest instead?

How should the register be funded?

Public finances are under unprecedented pressure at the moment, and there are no public funds set aside for a register. The Government proposes that the cost of running the register and meeting any ancillary costs arising from it should be met on a self-funding basis by the lobbying industry. Experience of other registers (see Annex A for examples) suggests that individual registration, in return for an initial and then annual registration fee, provides a practical and effective basis for funding a register.

The actual cost of running the register would depend on how many registrants there were, the range of information the register held, how often it was updated and what (if any) further responsibilities, such as the 'policing' of industry standards, the register's operator was given.

Do you agree that those involved in lobbying should fund the register? If not, why not, and what would be a better solution? At what levels might fees be set in order to effectively fund the register but not create an undue burden on the industry? Would this be affordable for small businesses? Should there be income-contingent fees to reduce the burden on businesses with small turnovers?

What sanctions would be appropriate?

Most regulatory regimes are backed by a range of sanctions, criminal and civil, to encourage compliance. In the United States, the penalties for failure to comply with the Lobbying Disclosure Act can be either a fine of up to $200,000 and/or imprisonment of up to five years. Under the Australian model, the only sanction available for non-compliance is deregistration. This has the effect of preventing a lobbyist from engaging in lobbying activities with Government representatives, but there are no other penalties available.

The Government hopes that the lobbying industry will embrace the register and take steps to make lobbying more transparent but believes that penalties should be available for non-compliance. Non-compliance might fall into a number of categories; not registering/refusing to register; registering late or not updating information or providing incorrect or incomplete information.

The Companies Act 2006 contains provisions in respect of the duty to file accounts and reports. These provisions might provide suitable benchmarks for any prospective offences in respect of the register of lobbyists. There are similarities between these duties and the proposals for the duty to register. Section 451 of the Act creates offences around *Default in filing accounts and reports*[4]. Failing to file accounts and reports by the required time can result in the company's directors receiving a fine of up to £5000. Knowingly or recklessly making a statement that is misleading, false or deceptive is a more serious offence that can result in higher fines, imprisonment of up to two years, or both[5].

The Government is interested in hearing your views on whether sanctions should apply to the duty to register. If so, what should they be, criminal or civil?

Who should run the register?

The Government aims to increase transparency and trust as a result of a register of lobbyists. Any increase in public trust will be in part dependent on whether the register is seen as reliable and

---

[4] Companies Act 2006, s451. Available at: http://www.legislation.gov.uk/ukpga/2006/46/section/451
[5] Companies Act 2006, s1112. Available at: http://www.legislation.gov.uk/ukpga/2006/46/section/1112

complete, as well as independent of the lobbying industry. One way to achieve this is for the register of lobbyists to be managed and enforced by a body which is independent of the lobbying industry, and also of Government.

Do you agree that the register should be managed and enforced by an independent body?

If you agree, there are a number of options as to who should operate the register:

- creating a new organisation expressly for this purpose;
- extending the remit of an existing Parliamentary body to take it on or
- extending the remit of a non-departmental public body to run the register.

Your views on the best solution are invited.

Whoever holds and operates the register, the Government believes that it should publish regular (at least annual) reports on its operation, including any difficulties encountered in ensuring it provides comprehensive and accurate information on lobbying.

What are your views on who should run the register?

5. Summary Of Questions

The key issues on which your views are invited are summarised below.

Definitions

- What definition of **lobbying** should be used?
- How should **lobbyists** be defined?

Scope

- Should lobbyists or firms acting on a pro bono basis be required to register?
- Should organisations such as Trade Unions, Think Tanks and Charities be required to register?
- How can public participation in the development of Government policy best be safeguarded?

Information to be included in the register

- Should the register include **financial information** about the cost of lobbying and about any public funding received?

Frequency of returns

- Should returns be required on a **quarterly** basis?

Additional functions

- Should the register's operator have any **additional functions** besides accurately reproducing and usefully presenting information provided by the registrants?

Funding

- Should the **lobbying industry meet the costs** of the register and any associated functions?

Sanctions

- Should **penalties** for non-compliance apply? If so, should they be broadly **aligned with those for offences under company law**?

The register's operator

- Who should run the register – a new body or an existing one? What sort of body should it be?

Annex A

1. Background

The Public Administration Select Committee (PASC) launched an inquiry into the Lobbying Industry in 2007, publishing a report in January 2009 which called for a statutory register of lobbying activity.[6]

In that report, PASC identified five key principles for a register of lobbying activity:

- It should be mandatory, in order to ensure as complete as possible an overview of activity.

- It should cover all those outside the public sector involved in accessing and influencing public-sector decision makers, with exceptions in only a very limited set of circumstances.

- It should be managed and enforced by a body independent of both Government and lobbyists.

- It should include only information of genuine potential value to the general public, to others who might wish to lobby government, and to decision makers themselves.

- It should include so far as possible information which is relatively straightforward to provide- ideally, information which would be collected for other purposes in any case.

The Committee additionally proposed that the following information would need to be provided by lobbyists and by the targets of their lobbying in order to abide by these principles:

- The names of the individuals carrying out lobbying activity and of any organisation employing or hiring them.

- In the case of multi-client consultancies, the names of their clients.

- Information about any public office previously held by an individual lobbyist.

---

[6] Lobbying: Access and Influence in Whitehall. Available from: www.publications.parliament.uk/pa/cm200809/cmselect/cmpubadm/36/36i.pdf

- A list of the relevant interests of decision makers within the public service (Ministers, senior civil servants and senior public servants) and summaries of their career histories outside the public service.

- Information about contacts between lobbyists and decision makers-essentially, diary records and minutes of meetings. The aim would be to cover all meetings and conversations between decision makers and outside interests.

The then Government's response,[7] published in October that year, did not accept the case for a statutory register, preferring more robust self-regulation instead, but did accept recommendations in other areas, mostly concerning the publication of meetings and hospitality received by senior civil servants and Ministers when dealing with interest groups.

The lobbying industry responded to the report by establishing the Public Affairs Council Working Party, chaired by Sir Philip Mawer, which was tasked to produce proposals for a self-regulatory body. In March 2010 the three main lobbying industry bodies – the Association of Professional Political Consultants, the Chartered Institute of Public Relations and the Public Relations Consultants Association – announced the creation of the UK Public Affairs Council (UKPAC), an independent not-for-profit body, to carry out four key functions:

- To maintain a Register of those engaged in lobbying and of the organisations on whose behalf they lobby;

- To hold and review periodically the Guiding Principles covering those who lobby, examining how a common Code of Conduct enshrining the Principles can be established and keeping under review any related Codes of member bodies;

- To oversee the disciplinary arrangements necessary to enforce the Principles and any common Code; to allocate complaints against individuals or organisations within member bodies to the most appropriate body; and to review periodically the process through which complaints are considered by member bodies; and

- To promote with its member bodies high ethical standards in lobbying generally.

UKPAC is overseen by a board comprising three independent members and three industry members. The three independent members were recruited by a process which complied with the principles of the Nolan rules for public appointments. The board is chaired by Elizabeth France CBE, one of its independent members. UKPAC's register is operational but is not yet fully populated. It is updated on a quarterly basis. The register can be viewed at www.publicaffairscouncil.org.uk.

UKPAC definition of lobbying

Lobbying means, in a professional capacity, attempting to influence, or advising those who wish to influence, the UK Government, Parliament, devolved legislatures or administrations, regional or local government or other public bodies on any matter within their competence.

---

[7] 'Lobbying: Access and Influence in Whitehall: Government response to the Committee's First Report of Session 2008-09. Available from: www.publications.parliament.uk/pa/cm200809/cmselect/cmpubadm/1058/1058.pdf

Lobbyists are those who, in a professional capacity, work to influence, or advise those who wish to influence, the institutions of government in the UK, in respect to:

- the formulation, modification or adoption of any legislative measure (including the development of proposals for legislation);

- the formulation, modification or adoption of a rule, regulation or any other programme, policy or position;

- the administration or execution of a governmental or other public programme or policy within the UK (including the negotiation, award or administration of a public contract, grant, loan, permit or licence).

Institutions of government means the UK Government, Parliament, the devolved legislatures or administrations, regional or local government or other public bodies.

The UKPAC definitions currently have effect in respect of a voluntary register, which is not backed by statute and which is not open to legal interpretation or challenge in the same way that a definition enshrined in law would be.

The Government believes this definition is unsuitable for use with a statutory register for a number of reasons:

- The concept of attempting to influence is extremely broad. Canadian experience in respect of the Lobbyists Registration Act suggests it is difficult to prove the intention behind actions. The more recent Lobbying Act refers more simply to communicating 'in respect of' legislation, policies and the like.

- Should a definition of lobbying include people or organisations advising those attempting to influence government, as the definition above does? An unintended consequence could be that, for example, lawyers advising lobbying companies on employment law or a building design expert helping a campaigning organisation to reduce its energy consumption might be required to register.

- Details of meetings between Ministers and businesses are already made public on www.data.gov.uk, along with details of other meetings with external organisations. The Government does not believe that there would be any notable increase in transparency by requiring companies lobbying on their own behalf to register.

Following the May 2010 election, the Coalition Government made a commitment to regulate lobbying through introducing a statutory register of lobbyists and ensuring greater transparency.

2. Examples of other jurisdictions' approaches to lobbying regulation

EUROPEAN PARLIAMENT AND COMMISSION

A joint (European Parliament and Commission) European Transparency register, building on earlier separate registers for the Parliament and Commission, was launched on 23 June 2011 in order to "register and monitor organisations and self-employed individuals engaged in EU policy-making and policy implementation". Registration is free and is not mandatory, except if seeking a pass to gain access to the premises of the European Parliament.

Scope

The scope of the register covers "all activities carried out with the objective of directly or indirectly influencing the formulation or implementation of policy and the decision-making processes of the EU institutions, irrespective of the channel or medium of communication used. Voluntary contributions and participation in formal consultations on envisaged EU legislative or other legal acts and other open consultations are also included."

A number of activities are excluded from the scope of the register, including legal advice, the activities of social partners (such as trade unions or trade associations) when they are playing an official role designated under a specific Treaty, activities in response to direct and individual requests from EU institutions or Members of the European Parliament, such as ad hoc or regular requests for factual information, data or expertise and/or individualised invitations to attend public hearings or to participate in the workings of consultative committees or in any similar forums.

There are also a number of exclusions for particular types of organisation, including churches and religious communities, political parties, local, regional and municipal authorities, although any representative offices or legal entities, offices and networks created to represent them, are expected to register.

Forms of collective activity (for example, networks) which have no legal status or legal personality but which constitute a source of organised influence and which are engaged in activities falling within the scope of the register are expected to register.

Registration is conditional on signing up to a code of conduct that requires transparency over who lobbyists are, who they represent and their aims and objectives. Registrants must keep their register entry accurate and up-to-date, act honestly and not seek to make others act dishonestly or in contravention of the rules and standards expected of them. They must also not claim any formal relationship with the EU or any of its institutions in their dealings with third parties.

Information requirements

Information must be updated at least annually. In addition to indicating the areas of policy in which they have an interest, registrants are required to provide a financial declaration. The areas it needs to cover depend on the type of organisation that is registering. Professional consultancies, law firms and self employed consultants are expected to disclose the turnover that results from activities falling within the scope of the register. Registrants must list their clients, presenting them in decreasing order of contract value (expressed in ranges). "In-house" lobbyists and trade or professional associations are expected to provide an estimate of the cost associated with the activities falling within the scope of the register. Other registrants (for example, NGOs and think-tanks) have to publish their overall budget, indicating their main sources of funding. All registrants must also declare any funding received from EU institutions.

Register operator

The Transparency Register Secretariat – a joint unit of the European Parliament and European Commission – operates the register.

Sanctions

Sanctions can be imposed for providing or failing to correct incomplete or inaccurate information in the register or for non-compliance with the code of practice. Sanctions include temporary suspension from the register or removal from it. In the case of removal, a one- or two-year ban on future registration can be applied. Removal can lead to the withdrawal of access privileges to the European Parliament.

UNITED STATES

The US has passed a number of laws to regulate lobbying. The central provision in respect of a lobbying register is contained in the Lobbying Disclosure Act (LDA) 1995, as amended by the Honest Leadership and Open Government Act 2007.

Scope

The LDA defines a lobbyist as any individual compensated by a client for services that include more than one lobbying contact (which guidance explains means more than one 'communication', and where there is an attempt to influence), except any whose lobbying activities constitute less than 20% of their time over a three-month period. A "client" is defined as any person or entity who employs and compensates another person to conduct lobbying activities on their behalf. Groups that carry out lobbying activities on their own behalf must also register.

Any lobbyist whose lobbying expenses exceed or are expected to exceed a specified threshold ($3000 over a quarterly period) is required to register once he or she has had a lobbying contact with senior members of the legislative or executive branches of the federal government, or with officials above a particular grade.

There are certain exclusions in respect of legal or investigative action.

Information requirements

The law requires lobbyists to file quarterly reports of their activities identifying the name of the registrant, the lobbyists the registrant employs, the client, the Houses of Congress and federal agencies contacted and the issues lobbied over. In addition, the disclosure must include:

- A 'good faith' estimate, by broad category (rounded to the nearest $10,000), of the total amount of lobbying-related income from the client, or expenditures by an organization lobbying in its own behalf, during the quarterly period;

- The specific issues that were the subject of a lobbyist's efforts, including "to the maximum extent practicable" a list of bill numbers;

- A statement of the houses of Congress and the federal agencies contacted by the lobbyist; and

- A list of the employees of the registrant who acted as lobbyists on behalf of the client, and a declaration of any previous employment as a covered executive branch or legislative branch official in the two years prior to registration.

Register operator

The register is operated by the Secretary of the Senate and the Clerk of the House of Representatives.

Sanctions

Criminal and civil penalties apply to deliberate violations of the Lobby Disclosure Act. In the case of a corrupt failure to comply, five years' imprisonment can result. For other violations, there can be a fine of up to $200,000

CANADA

Canada's first attempt at the regulation of lobbying was the Lobbyists Registration Act, which came into force in 1989. The 1989 Act provided for the public registration of individuals paid to lobby public office holders. However, it contained only basic requirements for lobbyists to register and provide information. Changes were made to clarify and strengthen its provisions, and to change the registrar's reporting lines, which had originally been to the government, to Parliament. It was comprehensively overhauled, becoming the Lobbying Act, in 2008.

Scope

The Act covers consultant lobbyists (people who are paid to lobby on behalf of clients) and two types of in-house lobbyists, in corporations (commercial businesses) and in organisations (not-for-profit organisations). In-house lobbyists are required to register only where lobbying is a significant part of their work. Guidance on the meaning of 'a significant part' of a person's duties explains that it is intended to cover those who spend more than 20% of their time on lobbying and/or the relative importance of lobbying in the context of their work.

There are exemptions for a variety of activities, including communications restricted to a straightforward request for publicly available information, the preparation and presentation of briefings to parliamentary committees, the making of submissions on behalf of employers in respect of the application or enforcement of federal laws and routine dealings with government inspectors and other regulatory authorities.

Information requirements

Information requirements include the names of lobbyists and their clients or organisations, the institutions being lobbied, the subjects of the lobbying and the methods used, details of any government funding received by the client/employer, information on lobbyists who used to hold public office and information on communications with certain public office holders, which includes virtually all those occupying an elected or appointed position in the Government of Canada, Members of Parliament and their staff, and the officers and employees of federal departments and agencies.

In addition to the initial information provided on registration, returns are required on a monthly basis in respect of any communications with designated public office holders, the key decision-makers within government. They include Ministers, senior official and senior members of the armed forces.

Returns must cover the name and title of the designated public office holder and the subject of the communication.

Register Operator

The Lobbying Act places the register under the control of the Office of the Commissioner of Lobbying of Canada. The Commissioner is an independent agent of Parliament responsible for educational programmes to improve public awareness of the Act's requirements as well as reviewing compliance.

Sanctions

Knowingly giving false or misleading statements in returns can result in a fine of up to $200,000 or two years' imprisonment. Other contraventions are punishable by a fine of up to $50,000.

AUSTRALIA

Australia's first attempt at the regulation of lobbying was the Lobbyists Registration Scheme, which was introduced in 1983. The Scheme set up two confidential registers: a special one for lobbyists representing foreign clients and a general one for lobbyists representing domestic clients. The Scheme required lobbyists to apply to register each time they took on a client and to give a short description of the task undertaken. As register lobbyists they were then required to produce a letter of acceptance from the Registrar whenever contacting minister or officials about this task. The Scheme was widely acknowledged to be ineffective, with its provisions rarely adhered to or enforced. The Scheme was abolished in 1996.

The Australian Government introduced a Lobbying Code of Conduct and a Register of Lobbyists in 2008. Government representatives are not allowed to engage (knowingly) in lobbying activities with unregistered individuals.

Scope

"Lobbying activities" means communications with a Government representative in an effort to influence Government decision-making, including the making or amendment of legislation, the development or amendment of a Government policy or program, the awarding of a Government contract or grant or the allocation of funding, but does not include:

- communications with a committee of the Parliament;

- communications with a Minister or Parliamentary Secretary in his or her capacity as a local Member or Senator in relation to non-ministerial responsibilities;

- communications in response to a call for submissions;

- petitions or communications of a grassroots campaign nature in an attempt to influence a Government policy or decision;

- communications in response to a request for tender;

- statements made in a public forum; or

- responses to requests by Government representatives for information.

"Lobbyist" means any person, company or organisation who conducts lobbying activities on behalf of a third party client or whose employees conduct lobbying activities on behalf of a third party client, but does not include:

- (a) charitable, religious and other organisations or funds that are endorsed as deductible gift recipients;

- (b) non-profit associations or organisations constituted to represent the interests of their members that are not endorsed as deductible gift recipients;

- (c) individuals making representations on behalf of relatives or friends about their personal affairs;

- (d) members of trade delegations visiting Australia;

- (e) persons who are registered under an Australian Government scheme regulating the activities of members of that profession, such as registered tax agents, Customs brokers, company auditors and liquidators, provided that their dealings with Government representatives are part of the normal day to day work of people in that profession; and

- (f) members of professions, such as doctors, lawyers or accountants, and other service providers, who make occasional representations to Government on behalf of others in a way that is incidental to the provision to them of their professional or other services. However, if a significant or regular part of the services offered by a person employed or engaged by a firm of lawyers, doctors, accountants or other service providers involves lobbying activities on behalf of clients of that firm, the firm and the person offering those services must register and identify the clients for whom they carry out lobbying activities.

Information requirements

The public Register of Lobbyists contains the following information about lobbyists who make representations to Government on behalf of their third-party clients:

> the business registration details and trading names of each lobbying entity including, where the business is not a publicly listed company, the names of owners, partners or major shareholders, as applicable;

> the names and positions of persons employed, contracted or otherwise engaged by the lobbying entity to carry out lobbying activities; and

> the names of clients on whose behalf the lobbying entity conducts lobbying activities.

Lobbyists are required to confirm or update their information every six months.

Register Operator

The Register is held and maintained by the Department of the Prime Minister and Cabinet, controlled by the Secretary of the Department of the Prime Minister and Cabinet.

Sanctions

Deregistration is the only current sanction available. The Australian Government consulted on amending the sanctions in 2010 and decided to leave the arrangements as they were.

3. UK Registers For Other Professions And Activities

A number of professional bodies, such as the General Dental Council, the General Medical Council, the Solicitors Regulation Authority and the Architects Registration Board carry out similar functions in respect of their professions.

For example, the **General Dental Council (GDC)** regulates dental professionals in the United Kingdom. All dentists, dental nurses, dental technicians, clinical dental technicians, dental hygienists, dental therapists and orthodontic therapists must be registered to work in the UK. The Dentists Act 1984 makes it a criminal offence, punishable by a fine of up to £5000, for anyone other than a registered dental professional to carry out dentistry. The GDC's functions include registering qualified professionals, setting standards of dental practice and conduct, assuring the quality of dental education, ensuring professionals keep up-to-date, helping patients with complaints about a dentist or dental care professional, and working to strengthen patient protection.

The GDC cost around £24m to run in 2010. It employed around 140 people, 44 of whom were concerned with maintaining the register. Initial and annual retention fees are charged for registration. They vary according to the type of work performed. Dentists must pay £576 per annum (pro rata if joining part-way through the registration year) and dental health professionals £120. There are exemptions for suitably qualified nationals of other European states.

Around 38,000 dentists and 57,000 dental care professionals were on the register in 2010. Around 1400 cases of problems regarding fitness to practise were considered during the year. Nearly 60 per cent went on for further investigation. Only two cases concerned practising while suspended from the register. Penalties ranged from being stuck off through to having conditions on practising imposed.

Ofsted has a very broad range of responsibilities, and cost around £180m to run in 2010/11. It regulates child care in a number of settings, including early years (children aged up to five) and general (older children) childcare. Both have registers. The general childcare register is split into a compulsory part for providers of childcare for children aged five to seven and a voluntary part for providers of childcare for children aged eight and over. Registrants must provide a range of information about their activities, including about their qualifications and state of premises, in order to secure registration. Childminders and child care providers cannot provide care before they receive their certificate of registration and once on the register they are subject to inspection by Ofsted. They can be deregistered if problems are detected and failure to comply with the registration rules can result in a fine of up to £5000.

In 2010/11, there were 83,739 providers on the Early Years Register. Ofsted inspects the quality of each provider at least once every four to five years, carrying out 17,500 during the year. Where problems are found, Ofsted re-inspects within a year to make sure improvements are taking place. There were 856 inspections of providers on the Childcare Register. These inspections took place on a random basis or when parents expressed concerns about the care provided

In 2010–11, Ofsted registered 7,503 new childminders and 2,261 childcare providers on domestic and non-domestic premises. It investigated 8750 complaints about childcare and children's social care services and in around half was able to secure improvements and compliance with law without using statutory enforcement action. Where providers are not able to meet the required standards or children are at risk of harm Ofsted has the power to suspend registration or to ultimately cancel registration. In 2010–11 Ofsted cancelled the registration of 39 providers and stopped them from operating. Ofsted opened 772 cases as a result of concerns received against registered and unregistered social care providers. In 470 cases it was able to secure improvements and compliance with the law without using statutory enforcement action, and set non-statutory actions in 141 cases. It served 13 enforcement notices (for unregistered provision) and welfare and statutory enforcement notices to ensure that unsuitable people were not looking after young people.

The Office of the Immigration Services Commissioner (OISC) regulates immigration advisers. Unpaid advisers are not required to register (they are 'listed' instead) but paid advisers are. As well as maintaining and publishing the register and list of advisers, the OISC regulates immigration advisers in accordance with its rules and the standards, receives complaints about immigration advisers, promotes good practice and prosecutes people operating outside the regulatory scheme.

Not all immigration advisers are regulated by OISC. Members of certain professional bodies (such as the Bar Council and Law Society) may give immigration advice without registering with OISC.

The OISC employed around 60 people during 2009/10 and cost around £4.2m to run. It charges registration fees (which apply only to paid immigration advisers), by reference to the type of work they do. Those providing the most basic level of advice are charged £595 for initial registration and subsequent continued registration. Organisations providing more complex services such as casework and advocacy pay fees that relate to the number of advisers employed. Those employing up to four advisers pay £1750 for the initial registration and £1290 for continued registration, those with five to nine £1960 and £1600 and larger organisations £2370 and £2115 respectively.

The total number of registered organisations in 2009/10 was 1733. 147 investigations were completed during the year. 26 convictions, with punishments including fines and prison sentences, and 9 cautions resulted.

Annex B: Code of Practice on Consultation

This document and the consultation process have been planned to adhere to the Code of Practice on Consultation, and are in line with the consultation criteria, which are:

- Formal consultation should take place at a stage when there is scope to influence policy outcome.

- Consultation should normally last for at least 12 weeks with consideration given to longer timescales where feasible and sensible.

- Consultation documents should be clear about the consultation process, what is being proposed, the scope to influence and the expected costs and benefits of the proposals.

- Consultation exercise should be designed to be accessible to, and clearly targeted at, those people the exercise is intended to reach.

- Keeping the burden of consultation to a minimum is essential if consultations are to be effective and if consultees' buy-in to the process is to be obtained.

- Consultation responses should be analysed carefully and clear feedback should be provided to participants following the consultation.

- Officials running consultations should seek guidance in how to run an effective consultation exercise and share what they have learned from the experience.